CW01665975

Toad Photographer

by BRIAN TRUEMAN

Book version by Nicholas Jones

Illustrations from the Cosgrove Hall production
Directed by Jackie Cockle

THAMES METHUEN

First published in Great Britain 1986
by Methuen Children's Books Ltd
11 New Fetter Lane, London EC4P 4EE
in association with Thames Television International Ltd
149 Tottenham Court Road, London W1P 9LL

Copyright © 1986 by Cosgrove Hall Productions Ltd

Book version © 1986 by Thames Television International Ltd
and Methuen Children's Books Ltd
Designed by Sue Ryall
Printed in Great Britain
ISBN 0 423 02000 5

The unabridged edition of THE WIND IN THE WILLOWS
by Kenneth Grahame is available with full colour illustrations
from the award-winning Cosgrove Hall production.

The Cosgrove Hall film of the original book
by Kenneth Grahame is available on Thames Video

Toad, Photographer

It was a glorious spring day, the first of the year with the high blue sky which foretold summer. Brilliant sunshine caught brilliant yellow dandelions in the meadows. Bracken uncurled like clock springs, and impatient bees shouldered their way into not-quite-yet-open cowslips in the shade of hedgerows.

Even Badger, underground in the Wild Wood, had felt the spring stirring. He had already sauntered down to Ratty, savouring the smell of the fresh greenness. The two of them had joined Mole and Toad for the first picnic of the year.

Ratty even allowed Mole and Toad to take the oars and row back to Toad Hall; Badger and Rat watched their efforts from the safety of the bank.

When they reached Toad Hall, afternoon tea awaited them. With *that* over, they sat back

contentedly, surrounded by the creamy, sugary, buttery, crumby, jammy debris.

'Well, I think you performed jolly well on the river, Toad,' Ratty said, smiling benvolently.

Toad had to agree. 'Yes, well I *am* . . . '

'. . . only losing the *one* oar!' finished Rat, wickedly.

'Yes!' agreed Toad, before he'd really taken in what Ratty had said. Then: 'Oh, I say!'

Conversation lapsed. In the pause, Mole gazed around him. It was a few months since he had been inside the Hall. Its elegance struck him afresh. 'My goodness, Toad! What a handsome home this is!'

Toad was not used to such unprompted praise from his friends. He tried to be modest. 'Eh? Oh, yes . . . it's not such a bad old place . . . '

'It's so grand!' Mole continued. 'And histori-cal! All those ancestors!'

'Yes.' For someone – particularly him – receiving such praise, Toad seemed strangely unenthusiastic. 'Mind you . . . ' he continued, 'I think there's something missing!'

'Missing, Toad?' queried Rat.

'It could do with . . . an addition . . . '

'I'm sorry, Toad?' Mole mused.

'Something *new* . . . '

This alarmed Badger, 'Now then, Toad! I promised your dear father that as long as I lived, I wouldn't let you knock this place about!'

But that was not Toad's meaning. 'No, no, Badger! I mean there's something missing from the *walls*!'

'Well, a pair of crossed oars would look rather splendid,' Ratty agreed, adding impishly '. . . or perhaps, in your case, just the one!'

Toad ignored the jibe. 'No, no! I mean a portrait!'

'A portrait, Toad?' Mole enquired.

'Whose portrait?' 'Whose . . . ? Why, mine, of course!'

'*Yours*, Toad?' said Badger reprovingly.

'Well, all the other famous Toads are up there! Look at them. And I expect I shall be much more famous than any of them.'

Ratty grinned and added: 'Or at least, notorious!' Badger simply said, 'Humph!'

Mole, as usual, was less censorious. 'No, I think Toad's right. He ought to be up there with the others. He *is* a Toad – as much as any of them.'

Badger could see the justice in this. 'Well . . . yes, Mole, you're quite right.'

The practical Rat was already thinking of how this was to be achieved. 'Where would you get one, Toad? Where would you have it done?'

Like so many of Toad's impulsive ideas, it had not been thought through. 'Ah! Well, erm . . . '

'Why couldn't Badger do it?' Mole suggested.

'What!?'

'Badger paints beautifully.'

'Nonsense! A dabbler!' Badger protested.

'Oh, come on Badger old man!' said Ratty, brushing aside the objection. 'You know you do!'

Toad, although he admired Badger's work, was not sure. 'Er . . . I mean . . . I know that Badger is a genius with the brush and all that . . . '

'Herrumph!' said the embarrassed object of this praise.

'. . . but it's just that I am – not that it's any credit to *me* – just a gift of nature you understand . . . I am unusually . . . ' He paused. The others looked at him cautiously. What was he about to say? Could he really be as boastful as they feared . . .

'. . . handsome!' Toad finished. Yes. He could.

Badger groaned. Rat and Mole looked at each other and smiled. This was the old Toad they knew. They had thought, after his generosity with the Christmas Hamper, that perhaps . . . But no. Toad was in full flight:

'I just wouldn't like any detail to be lost. I mean it wouldn't be fair to my successors.'

Badger ignored the conceit, and said practically,

'If you want to capture your features perfectly, Toad, perhaps you should have a photographic study.'

Rat was enthusiastic: 'I say, that's a good idea – you've seen Badger's photographs, Toad?'

Toad pondered. No, he thought. That wasn't in keeping with all the other portraits. He said so. 'Surely that's not quite the thing for a *gentleman's* portrait.'

Mole knew a little about these things. 'Well . . . perhaps you're right, Toad. But my cousin Auberon has just had his likeness photographed, and he says it's very fashionable and all the rage.'

These words were music to Toad's ears.

'Fashionable . . . ' 'All the rage . . . ' Maybe there was something in it after all.

The others could see how Toad's mind was working. 'Tush, man!' said Badger quickly. But not quickly enough. Toad was in a brown study. Rat and Badger saw that it was too late. 'Oh no!' they said. Toad began to think aloud:

'Of course, I wouldn't want an *old, half*-plate camera . . . '

Mole saw what he had started. 'Oh dear!'

'. . . No! I shall have the very latest *whole*-plate camera! And side plates too!' Rat and Badger groaned. '. . . First thing in the morning, I'll motor into London . . . '

'Now, look here, Toad!' Badger tried to interpose.

'. . . and get myself a camera! Or two!'

Rat's face was so expressive that he scarcely had to speak, but he did say, 'It's no use, Badger.

He's off again. It's another craze!'

'Oh, dear!' said Mole, 'It's all my fault!'

'No, no, Mole,' soothed Rat. 'If it hadn't been photography, it would have been something else . . .'

Badger nodded in agreement. 'Foolish creature!'

'It'll be like a fever, now,' continued Rat. 'We'll just have to let it burn itself out!'

'Oh dear, oh dear!' muttered the contrite Mole.

Amidst this discussion, Toad continued his reverie. 'Click! click! click! I shall immortalise my friends . . . my house . . . *myself*!'

* * *

First thing in the morning, Toad went to order the cameras which, he thought, would bring him permanent fame. It seemed an age to him, as he awaited their arrival, but then, four days later,

he was awoken by a delivery rabbit knocking on the door of Toad Hall. 'Mr Toad?'

'That's me!'

'Packages for yer! Sign 'ere please!'

'Oh, yes! Ah ha! *Thank* you!'

Toad dragged the packages into the hall and attacked the wrappings. A few impatient minutes later, he was surrounded by all the accoutrements of a master photographer.

He tossed aside the instruction book so thoughtfully provided by the camera makers: *'Photography for Novices!'* he said, contemptuously. *'Novices!* I shall be a Fellow of the Royal . . . er . . . . Photographic Society by the end of the week. *Novices* indeed! Now, where to begin my breathtaking career . . . !'

* * *

Clearly, he decided, the first thing to immortalise was his noble home. He retreated down the drive for a few yards, and set up the tripod . . . or rather, tried to. Were he a snake-wrestler at the circus, his antics might have been expert. They were certainly not those of an expert *photographer*. 'Waagh! Ooof! Oh, bother!' He tripped over a leg, and fell over, bringing the camera down on top of him. He tried again, and was just about to take the photograph when the entire apparatus subsided gracefully to the ground, catching his finger in a hinge, 'Ouch! Oooh! Tcha!'

But eventually, having succeeded in taming the camera, he managed to look through it for the first time. After a moment or two, a muffled voice came from under the cloth. He hadn't realised the camera would show the picture upside down, and that he would have to allow for it.

'Eh?! Oh, drat! Oh, bother and blow! Useless! Stupid shop-keeper! The picture's upside down! Junk! Absolute junk . . . ! Ah! Wait a minute!' And he turned the camera upside down on the tripod. 'Good job *some* of us have some intelligence!'

This, of course, made no difference, and Toad decided that the only solution was to look between his legs, with *him* upside down. Success! 'Ha ha! Got it!' In his jubilation, he forgot that he was at the top of a flight of steps. He edged back a little too much, and . . . crash!

Rubbing his bruises, he went to fetch the spare camera he had so fortunately ordered.

* * *

Toad was evidently going to be as profligate with cameras as he was with cars. During the next few days, his friends had their patience sorely tried, as Toad insisted on photographing them. For instance, he arrived one morning to take a picture of Rat outside his riverside home. After twenty minutes of trial and error – largely error – Rat was exasperated:

'Look, Toad, I can't hang about much longer!'

'Perfection, my dear Rat, takes time! As I'm sure Badger's old father *must* have said!'

'Huh!'

As he spoke, Toad was moving gradually further away from his subject. 'I can't *quite* get you *and* your nice little home in at the same time . . .' He moved a little more.

Rat could see impending disaster. 'Er . . . Toad . . . ! Toad!' His calls became more urgent as Toad neared the river's edge.

'Please, Ratty! You're disturbing my– waagh!'

Splash! Toad bobbed gently up and down in the water. So did the camera, floating away downstream.

After he had clambered out, the bedraggled animal said woefully, 'Oh dear! I think I'd better pop up to town in the morning!' Unlike most photographers, who need regular supplies of film, plates or developer, *Toad* needed cameras. Four days later found the delivery rabbit on a second visit. The day after that Mole was subject to Toad's ineptitude . . .

'Oh dear, Toad! I'd really rather not. My little home isn't . . .'

'Nonsense. I shall make it famous! "See Mole's humble residence as photographed by Toad!" '

'But I'm halfway through getting dinner ready!'

Mole might not have spoken for all the effect it had. Toad refused to listen. 'Mind you, it's a bit dark in here. Hang on a minute while I set up the . . . er . . . flash thingy . . . '

'Now!' There was a blinding flash; the room filled with smoke.

But Toad was at last satisfied, and he left with instructions that Mole should come to Toad Hall the next day to see the results – 'never will you have seen such slides!'.

* * *

Toad had prevailed upon Badger to loan his magic lantern for the occasion, and it was set up in the great hall. Toad was preparing his audience, building their anticipation:

'. . . and I've got them all in order so that you can enjoy them properly!'

'Have they come out well, Toad?' Mole asked innocently.

'Come out . . . ? Of course they'll have come out well!'

The future tense made Badger suspicious. 'Toad . . . ?'

'Why, when I take a photograph . . . ! Yes, Badger?'

'You have *looked* at these slides of yours?'

'Erm . . . well, actually . . . er . . . no!'

'But, Toad . . . !' Rat began.

'Well, what's the point? I *know* how good they are!' said Toad, brightly. Badger groaned. Toad continued, 'I didn't want to spoil the absolute thrill of seeing my creative genius writ large upon the shimmering screen!'

'My word, Toad,' said Rat, 'you *have* got it bad!'

Badger was resigned. 'Yes, well . . . better get on with it, then!' He crossed over to his projector, while Toad concerned himself with his audience:

'Now, are you all comfortable? I mean, you can see the screen all right?'

'Yes, thank you, Toad!' said the other three, somewhat wearily.

'Only I wouldn't like you to miss any of the—'

'Toad!' Badger silenced the voluble animal.

'Oh . . . yes, Badger!'

'We shall commence.'

'Ahem. Yes,' said Toad. 'Well, the first one is the stately façade of Toad Hall . . . '

Badger moved the slide carrier. The room remained in blackness.

'*Thank* you, Badger!' Toad said impatiently. 'Badger?'

'That, Toad, is it!'

'*It*!?'

'You didn't, by any chance, leave the lens cap on?'

'Lens cap? Lens cap!' exclaimed Toad indignantly, then, *soto voce*, 'Ah! So that's what it wa . . . No!' Then louder again, 'No! Of course not. It's . . . er . . . an *experimental* photograph. Erm . . . Toad Hall by . . . er . . . night! Now, the next one is a self-portrait. Ha! I fancy this will look handsome on the wall. There! Thank you, Badger!'

A picture appeared on the screen. It was in focus, and well exposed . . . and showed the bottom half of Toad's face, and his body down to the knees.

'Yes, Toad!' agreed Rat. 'As handsome as I've ever seen you!'

Mole was overcome by unseemly laughter . . . which Toad found inexcusable. 'Mole! I say, Mole!'

'I'm . . . hee, hee! . . . sorry, Toad!'

'Yes, well,' replied the only-partly-mollified Toad. 'That was just a try-out. This next one is the one I meant.'

And a picture of Toad – from knees to feet – appeared on screen.

'Jolly good, Toad,' said Rat, jovially. 'We only

need the top of your head and we've got the set.'

Mole giggled helplessly.

'It's those wretched developing people!' said Toad, wildly. 'They've done 'em all wrong!'

'Nonsense, Toad!' said Badger. 'Next!'

'Oh, well, it's . . . er, one I took of Rat in his boat!'

The slide appeared. The intention was clear. The stern of the boat, unmistakably clear. But Rat . . . No!

'Erm . . . ah!' said Toad, 'He's . . . er . . . just off to the right. Wonderful sense of movement, don't you think . . . !'

Mole collapsed in helpless laughter. 'Mole!' exclaimed Toad, increasingly irritated, 'I do wish you'd stop that!'

Badger simply said 'Next!' in a voice which brooked no argument.

Toad began to have doubts. 'Look, Badger, er . . . How about . . . '

'Next!'

'Oh, go on then,' said Toad, glumly, shifting uneasily in his chair. When he had said to Mole that 'never will you have seen such slides', this wasn't quite what he had meant. Some were out of focus, some had Toad's fingers over the lens; some had simply missed the subject altogether. Toad squirmed in discomfort. Badger went remorselessly on. Rat grinned. Mole laughed helplessly.

At last, Badger announced, 'And that, Toad, is the last of your masterpieces!'

Whilst intensely relieved, Toad was also disappointed. 'Oh! Not one! No landscapes . . . no riverscapes . . . and no portrait of me!'

'Oh, that *is* a pity,' said Rat, chuckling ironically. 'I suppose you haven't got any photographs you can show us, Badger?'

'Didn't I see you taking some at Toad Hall, Badger?' Mole added, knowing the answer full well. On cue, Badger replied with measured modesty: 'Well, yes. I do have one or two if you would care to see them. Only taken with my *old* camera of course. Yes, in fact, I think there may be *one* of you, Toad.

'Ha ha! Looking pretty dashing and handsome, eh!'

Badger pondered a moment. 'Hmmm! Well, it certainly looks like *you*!'

Rat was impatient. 'Well, come on, Badger! Don't keep us in suspense!'

'Absolutely not!' Toad agreed.

Badger had an actor's sense of timing. He waited a moment more, then: 'Oh, very well . . . There!'

A superb action shot appeared on the screen: Toad falling down the steps. Rat and Mole laughed heartily, whilst Toad protested. 'Oh! I say!'

Realising that older methods might have their advantages after all, Toad asked Badger if he would *paint* his portrait. A bright morning a few days later therefore found the friends on the terrace of Toad Hall : Toad was holding a suitably noble pose, Badger stood ready with palette and brushes. Rat and Mole watched, intrigued.

'You won't miss my dimple, will you?' Toad remarked, as lightly as he could.

'Toad!' Badger needed to say no more.

'Oh, all right!'

' "Vanity will prove vexation," my old father used to say – and by Jove he was right!'

Mole wandered over to the easel to examine Badger's progress. 'Oh my! It's ever so good!' He sighed. 'I can only paint *walls*! But imagine being a Rembrandt, or Tintoretto, or Gainsborough!'

Rat could scarecly believe Mole would risk such a remark in Toad's hearing. 'Mole!' he said, a warning note in his voice. It was unheeded. 'Goodness me, one would be so famous. *Everyone* would want you to paint things!'

'Mole!' said Ratty, rather more sharply.

But Toad had heard this last remark. 'Eh? Famous . . . ? I think I might take a little trip to town this afternoon . . .'

'Toad!' cried Rat and Badger together.

'Of course, *I'd* need a *bigger* easel . . . and a *very* big box of paints . . .'

Badger and Rat looked at each other and groaned.

Mole could only wonder how he could have been so careless.